mini EXPLORERS

Pirates

Written by: Kirsty Neale
Illustrated by: Laszlo Vere

igloo

What is a Pirate?

A pirate is someone who attacks and robs another ship at sea. Pirates have been around for thousands of years, stealing anything of value from enemy ships, and often killing the crew.

▶ The Pirate Round was a sailing route followed by many pirates in the 1600s and 1700s. Ships sailed from the Caribbean Sea across the Atlantic Ocean, around Africa and on to the Indian Ocean.

Barbary corsairs were pirates from North Africa who sailed in the Mediterranean Sea. They attacked **merchant ships**.

Women were not allowed on board ship, so female pirates, such as Mary Read, dressed as men to disguise themselves.

In some parts of the world, such as

Caribbean
Sea

Africa

Indian
Ocean

N
E
S

► Pirates
of the
Caribbean
were called
buccaneers. They
attacked Spanish
ships carrying
treasure back to
Spain from
Mexico.

the South China Seas, pirates still exist!

A Pirate ship

Galleons and **brigantines** were big ships that could survive tough battles and long voyages. Smaller, faster ships, such as **sloops** and **schooners**, didn't travel as far but were good at making surprise attacks.

stern (back) of the ship

captain's cabin

rudder

▲ The captain ate his meals and gave orders to the crew from his cabin, which was the most comfortable part of the ship.

cannons

A pirate crew usually outnumbered

If there was no wind, a ship's sails were no use, so some pirate ships carried lots of oars. In calm weather, the crew could keep the ship moving by rowing it.

rigging

bow (front) of the ship

oars

A ship's boat was used to reach nearby enemy ships, or to row to the shore.

the sailors on a merchant ship.

The Captain and Crew

A pirate captain decided where the ship would sail, and gave orders during battle. The crew worked hard and if they stuck to the Ship's Articles, or rules, they got a share of any captured treasure.

The ship's surgeon often had to cut off a pirate's arm or leg if it was badly injured in an attack or storm.

The cabin boy acted as a pirate captain's servant. He delivered messages, laid out the captain's clothes and served his meals.

Most pirates had just one set o

▶ Sir Francis Drake was an English captain who attacked Spanish ships when England was at war with Spain. Sailors who did this were known as **privateers**.

▼ The quartermaster was the captain's second-in-command. He took charge of **rations**, inspected weapons and directed the gunners.

quartermaster

gunners

clothes, which they hardly ever washed.

Pirate Grub

Pirate ships had to carry enough food for long journeys. If the men went too long without vegetables and fruit, they got scurvy, a disease that causes teeth to drop out.

Sailors sometimes caught fish or sea turtles. These were used in a stew, called salmagundi.

Really hungry pirates sometimes ate

◀ The ship's cook rubbed salt into meat and vegetables to make them last longer. Spices were added to cover up the taste of rotten food.

Foods

When there was nothing else left, pirates ate dry biscuits, known as hard-tack, and drank rum. The cook sometimes made soup from fish or rat bones.

hard-tack with **weevils**

bone soup

rum

Animals were often carried on long voyages. Chickens provided eggs and pigs were kept for their meat.

Rats ate sailors' food and spread diseases. Many ships kept a cat on board to catch and kill the rats.

...ats, or even birds that landed on deck.

The two **masts** on a brigantine were supported by an arrangement of ropes, called rigging.

Setting Sail

Every pirate had to know how to repair sails and keep the ship watertight. They took it in turns to sail the ship, or act as lookout in the **crow's nest**.

◀ To change course, sailors had to climb the rigging and adjust the sails.

Many pirates believed that whistling

Any holes in a ship were filled with pieces of old rope and **pitch**, which sets hard like tar, to make the repair waterproof.

Sewing was an important skill for pirates. They made their own flags and had to repair sails that were torn in battle or strong winds.

▼ It took many sailors to raise the ship's anchor, using a type of pulley called a **capstan**. They often sang sea shanties, or songs, as they worked.

n board a ship would bring bad luck.

Steering a Course

Pirate voyages sometimes lasted several years. It was important to work out the ship's position, route and speed to keep the boat on course and safe from danger.

telescope

sextant

▼ A telescope allowed sailors to see land and other ships from a long way away.

Navigation instruments were very
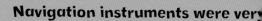

▶ The captain plotted the ship's position on a chart. He used dividers to work out how far the ship had moved each day.

globe

◀ The **navigator** relied on an instrument called a sextant to work out the ship's exact location.

dividers

chart

Instruments

Speed at sea is measured in knots. Sailors dropped a knotted line with a wooden weight at the end over the side of the ship to work out how fast the ship was moving. A compass showed the direction in which the ship was sailing.

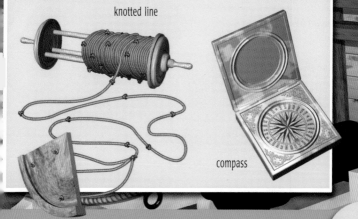

knotted line

compass

expensive, so pirates often stole them.

Fighting the Enemy

A pirate ship needed to get close to the enemy quickly, without being seen. Pirates kept their weapons clean and sharp, so they were ready to attack.

tricorn, or three-cornered, hat

sword

Blackbeard was a terrifying English pirate. He fought using a sword and pistols.

▼ A pirate flag was called a Jolly Roger. This one was Blackbeard's design.

pistol, also used as a club

To scare people, Blackbeard tucked

Weapons

Pirates used **grenades** filled with exploding **gunpowder**. The gunpowder was stored in barrels. They also used chain-shot – two cannonball halves joined by a chain. Chain-shot ripped through an enemy's sails, so the ship could not escape.

grenade

chain-shot

barrels of gunpowder

A Jolly Roger often featured a skull and crossbones, which were recognized and feared by sailors everywhere. Pirates would raise their flag as soon as they were spotted by another ship.

skull

crossbones

fiery pieces of rope into his long beard.

Treasure!

Pirates stole many kinds of treasure, from coins and jewels to weapons and medicines. The best **loot** was an enemy's ship. Treasure was divided up fairly between the captain and crew.

Silver coins were looted from Spanish galleons. The coins were worth eight smaller coins in Spanish currency, so pirates called them 'pieces of eight'.

Most pirates spent their treasure

▲ A rich passenger was sometimes captured and held to **ransom**. If the ransom wasn't paid, the person was killed or put to work on the pirate ship.

In the Mediterranean Sea, Barbary corsairs captured their enemies and sold them as slaves in the markets, making even more money for their treasure chests.

Punishments

If a pirate broke the rules in the Ship's Articles, he was punished by the captain. Some pirates were flogged, or whipped, while the unluckiest were **marooned** on a desert island and left to die.

▼ Any pirate who was caught faced death by hanging. His body was displayed near the seashore as a warning to others not to turn to piracy.

A few very cruel pirates blindfolded victims, tied their hands together and made them walk along a plank until they fell into the sea.

In a 'heave to' punishment, victims

▼ A cat o' nine tails was a whip made from nine lengths of knotted rope. It was used to flog disobedient pirates.

cat o' nine tails

captain

▲ If a crew thought their captain was acting unfairly, they punished him and voted for a new person to become captain.

were picked up and thrown overboard.

Glossary

Brigantine
A ship with two masts and square sails on the front mast.

Capstan
Equipment used to pull up, or hoist, a heavy object using a rope.

Crow's nest
A platform at the top of a ship's mast used as a lookout point.

Galleon
A large sailing ship with three or four masts, used by the Spanish from the 15th to the 17th centuries to carry goods.

Grenade
A small bomb, thrown by hand.

Gunpowder
A mixed powder that explodes when it is lit by a flame.

Loot
Stolen goods.

Marooned
Left in a place, such as an island, from which you can't escape.

Mast
The tall pole that supports the sails of a ship.

Merchant ship
A ship used to carry cargo and passengers from one country to another.

Navigator
A person who is able to plan a ship's course and work out its position at sea.

Pitch
A thick, sticky, tar-like substance that sets hard and is used to make boats waterproof.

Privateer
A pirate who worked for the government, attacking enemy ships, usually while countries were at war with each other.

Ransom
A large sum of money demanded in return for setting a prisoner free.

Ration
The amount of food that a person is allowed.

Schooner
A sailing ship with two masts.

Sloop
A small sailing boat with one mast.

Weevils
Name used for the wriggly, maggot-like insects found in ship's biscuits, or hard-tack.